THE
OPENERS & CLOS
POCKETBOOK

By Alan Evans and Paul Tizzard

Drawings by Phil Hailstone

"A great source of practical, adaptable ideas for creating good learning states and for setting the pace and tone of really great training. A must for every busy trainer, facilitator and team leader."
Graham Watson, Interim Manager, CIPD Training

Published by:
Management Pocketbooks Ltd
Laurel House, Station Approach, Alresford, Hants SO24 9JH, U.K.
Tel: +44 (0)1962 735573   Fax: +44 (0)1962 733637
E-mail: sales@pocketbook.co.uk
Website: www.pocketbook.co.uk

This edition published 2005.

© Alan Evans and Paul Tizzard 2005.

British Library Cataloguing-in-Publication Data.   A catalogue record for this book is available
from the British Library.

ISBN 1 903776 30 9

Design, typesetting and graphics by **efex ltd**. Printed in U.K.

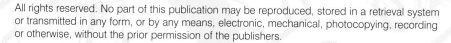

CONTENTS

FOREWORD BY DR. PETER HONEY

I'd hate to calculate how many days of my life have been spent running courses of various kinds. This isn't because I have any particular regrets - just that it wouldn't serve any useful purpose (and might even trigger morbid thoughts about how many days remain!).

All the courses I have run shared two characteristics: they were riddled with beginnings and endings. In addition to the actual beginning and end, each session had a beginning and an end and each day had a beginning and an end – even each morning and afternoon had beginnings and ends. Each beginning was vital because it set the tone for everything that followed. Each end was vital because it rounded things off, like a full stop at the end of a sentence. Needless to say, the actual ending was also vital since it heralded the transition from the temporary haven created by the course to the real world.

So, beginnings and endings are not to be taken lightly. They matter – and there are lots of them on every course. This book will leave you in no doubt about why they matter and why it is worth investing time to create purposeful beginnings and ends.

Besides the sheer ingenuity of many of the ideas in this book, I particularly like the way the authors urge you to forge strong links between the opening and/or closing activity and the course content itself. Anyone can dream up unrelated activities; the trick is to make them relevant to the learning content.

I also applaud the suggestion that you should adapt the material and make it your own. I have always been hopeless at regurgitating other people's materials like an actor speaking someone else's lines. Much better, in my experience, to pinch the germ of an idea and adapt and modify it. This book gives you ample opportunities to do just that.

Dr Peter Honey

December 2004

INTRODUCTION

OUR PHILOSOPHY & APPROACH

Welcome to the Openers & Closers Pocketbook. This book will give you a wide range of original, quick ideas and activities to use to open and close your courses, or sessions within your courses.

We have written this book with the busy trainer in mind. Each opener or closer has been specially designed to get your groups energized and thinking about the subject matter straight away.

We believe that training sessions of any description should be memorable and put the point across in a punchy way. We also believe that icebreakers should be linked in subject to the course that you are running. That way, you not only help people get to know each other and energize them, but you also get them thinking about the course itself so that they learn quicker. It is also important to say that we want you to adapt these ideas to however you want to work with them, and make them your own.

INTRODUCTION

FINDING THE RIGHT OPENER & CLOSER

The activities contained in the book are either generic, for use on any type of course, eg the rapport-building icebreakers, or recommended for particular subjects, eg the bangs and subject openers.

The openers and closers fall into the following categories:
- Beginning of course action planning
- Rapport-building icebreakers
- Opening and closing bangs (mixture of pithy stories, metaphors and analogies)
- Short snappy activities
- Climate checkers

Most of the suggestions can be used either to open or close sessions. We leave it to you to use your own judgment as to what would best suit your courses.

We have not specified the time needed for the activities, as they are meant to be quick to use. As you work with them, you can choose to lengthen them if your groups are responding well.

IN SHORT...

Our **openers** will help you to:
- Merely *break the ice* or
- Arouse interest in your topic or,
- A mixture of both (plus have some fun too)

Our **closers** will help you to:
- Use some different ways to end the course and make pledges to action
- Review a topic in a way that will make it more memorable!

Have fun and get them learning as quickly as you can!

Disclaimer. To the best of our knowledge, all of these openers and closers are original. Any similarity to material already available is entirely unintentional.

TAG-ONS

WHAT ARE TAG-ONS?

We use Tag-ons to add to the technique known by trainers as the *paired interview*. The technique is defined as a low energy, low risk way of introducing a course. We nearly always start with this technique because we know how anxious delegates can feel at the beginning of a course. We believe it is essential to build rapport before anyone will listen to you, let alone learn from you.

Paired technique

Say something like, 'In pairs, introduce yourselves to one another by answering the questions on the flipchart. After ten minutes, please introduce each other to the rest of the group.' Examples of questions are below. The Tag-on is the final question which introduces a touch of quirkiness to the whole proceedings.

Questions:

1. Who are you?
2. Where do you work/what do you do?
3. What is it you want from this course today?
4. **Tag-on (see next page for examples)**

TAG-ONS

EXAMPLES

Quite simply, Tag-ons are a light-hearted way of getting delegates to reveal a little bit of *what makes them tick* – without asking them directly. The selections below are not linked to specific courses. When you create your own, we suggest that if you can link the Tag-on question to the course content in some way, it will have greater impact.

Record breakers!	*What record would you like to break if time/money/fitness etc were no object?*
Inventions	*What do you think is the greatest ever invention? Why?*
History	*Pick a time in history you would like to have lived in. Say why.*

EXAMPLES

| **Soapy** | *If you were a soap star who would you be?*
Or: Which soap would you most like to appear in as yourself?
What would be your part? What would you say/do? |

| **Mr. Men** | *Pick a Mr. Man or Little Miss character that you think best represents your personality. Say why.* |

| **Transporter** | *If you were a mode of transport, what would you be?* |

| **Three things**
(more general) | *Name three things that you want from the course.*
Name three things that you can offer everyone else on the course.
Name three facts about yourself that in some way relate to this course. |

RAPPORT-BUILDING ICEBREAKERS

RAPPORT-BUILDING ICEBREAKERS

INTRODUCTION

The aim of this section is to get delegates talking to each other in a fairly focused manner. These activities work by *breaking the ice* without the trainer having to say, in some contrived manner, 'Well, here is the icebreaker!'. Which, as you know, is almost the kiss of death at this stage.

We find that these work best if you use them pretty quickly after the paired interview technique mentioned earlier, or as an opener to a session at any point during the course itself. You will also find that some will work better with different types of groups, but all favour action over inaction. As we always say, though, take time to adapt them to suit your own personality and style of training.

RAPPORT-BUILDING ICEBREAKERS

DICEY!

Summary
Participants volunteer personal information to accelerate rapport between one another, using dice as a prompt.

Materials
One or two big dice (see www. thetrainingshop.co.uk for ideas).

Process
1. Take your dice and invite the participants to join you in a space in the room.
2. Pair the participants together (use three's if you have a large group).
3. Explain that this activity is just a bit of fun to accelerate the process of getting to know one another. Say that you will throw the dice against the wall and call out a number from 1 to 12. Their task, with their partner(s), is to discuss and come up with a piece of personal information which relates to the number, and then to share this information with the group, eg: 'I have six kids' or 'I was three when the Berlin Wall came down'.
4. Any information volunteered, and linked to the number rolled, wins the pair a point – and points mean prizes!

Process (cont'd)

5. Note the names of the pairs on the flipchart.
6. Throw the dice.
7. The delegates are to call out anything they can, related to the number showing.
8. For each pair who manage to make a link, log a point next to their names on the flipchart.
9. Throw the dice again several times until everyone has had a chance to volunteer something.
10. Add up the points and issue a cheesy prize to the winners (or play safe and have a cheesy prize for all!)

What's the point?

Apart from being a fun way to build rapport, this activity is a superb way to get people talking without making them feel *on the spot*. Each roll of the dice, with its accompanying answers from participants, provides both you the trainer and the other participants with an opportunity to question and probe further upon answers provided. Eg, 'When I was seven I had my first guitar lesson' may lead to, 'Really, how good did you get? What made you choose the guitar at that age? Who taught you?' etc. This approach is light-hearted, informal and takes the starch out of nervous introductions.

Variation

Ask the participants to decide upon the criteria for the quality of the answers, eg funniest, most amazing, saddest, most inspiring, weirdest, etc. Allocate a prize to the pair voted as having volunteered the best quality answer.

Variation as a closer

Use the dice to ask participants to relate what they have learnt from the course to the numbers that they roll. For example, 'I've rolled six which was the number of stages it takes to build a project from scratch...'

TIMELINE

Summary
Participants use a physical timeline to share a visual overview of the major significant events of their lives.

Materials
Ball of string, A4 or A5 paper, Blu-Tack, Post-it® pads, scissors, marker pens (enough for everyone) **or** flipchart and pens.

Process
1. Hand out a piece of string and two pieces of A4 or A5 paper to each participant.
2. Ask them to write **Birth** on one piece of paper and **Present** on the other.
3. Give each participant a lump of Blu-Tack and ask them to stick their timeline somewhere in the room where it will be seen (flat on the wall / corner to corner on the wall / floor / ceiling / door), with Birth at one end and Present at the other.
4. Hand out a pad of Post-it® notes and a marker pen to each participant and inform them that their task is to litter their timeline with particularly outstanding or significant events/experiences from their lives so far.

Process (cont'd)
5. Then choose one of these approaches:
   - Pair the delegates up and ask them to share the meaning behind their timeline
   - Ask each pair to introduce their partner
   - Ask participants to wander around *gallery style* and ask about each other's timelines
   - Ask participants to pair up with someone new whenever you call time (use five minute intervals to keep it snappy)
   - Ask each participant in turn to introduce their own timeline to the group

Caution
We think the trainer should demonstrate their own timeline first to set the tone. There is a chance that people may get emotional when taking part in this activity. This is normal as some people feel more able than others to share their emotions, but if you are concerned about this happening, don't use this icebreaker.

 Continued

What's the point?

This is a safe and visual way of conducting introductions. It is memorable and fun, and helps build lasting rapport early on.

Variation

If you want to use this as a subject-focused opener it works well on personal development programmes.

RAPPORT-BUILDING ICEBREAKERS

'ME' CARD

Summary
Participants compete in an attempt to link sets of life events/facts to the participants they think most probably own them.

Materials
Pre-prepared cards, name badges (stickers will do), prizes, eg individually wrapped sweets (optional).

Process
1. As each delegate arrives, ask them to wear a clearly labelled name badge.
2. Hand to each person a card with several headings, eg Like, Hate, Hobbies, Most Entertaining Moment, Greatest Achievement, Last Job, Biggest Faux Pas, etc.
3. Ask them to fill in the card without letting anyone know/see their answers.
4. Collect in the cards and number them.

Continued

Process (cont'd)

5. Tell the delegates that they have ten minutes, before you read the cards out, to move around the room *cocktail party style* finding out as much as they can about other people prior to the competition.

6. Say 'Go!'. (Generate a sense of urgency/competition by saying things like: 'Four minutes left'…'Now two!' etc). Call time after ten minutes.

Process (cont'd)
7. Ask the delegates to sit and write on a piece of paper a numbered list from one – xx (the number of participants in the room)
8. Read out the details of each numbered card in sequence. Ask everyone to write down the name they believe it belongs to – until everyone has a name next to each number.
9. Once all the cards have been read, ask the participants to swap papers with the person next to them, ready for marking (you'll have no cheating!)
10. Re-read each card, get a general impression of who thought what, then ask the owner to reveal themselves. Participants allocate ticks or crosses to the paper they are marking.
11. Find out who had the most correct answers, and reward them with applause, prizes or whatever you like.

What's the point?
Trainers often forget how scary it can be to come in to a room full of strangers, or how much effort and time it can take to build rapport with people. Anyone worrying about this will be feeling a little stressed, and as a result is less likely to learn anything.
This activity is light-hearted and a great way for participants to get to know the whole group early on.

Variation

- Hand the numbered cards back – one to each delegate
- Tell them not to show the card to anyone else
- Ask them to move around the room asking questions until they believe they have found the owner of the card
- Once they believe they have found the owner, they should write the person's name on the card, without revealing who they think it is
- Ask each person to read out their card details and reveal who they think it is
- Allocate sweets to all correct answers
- Alternatively, ask them to work in pairs or groups

Variation as a closer

Use it at the end of the course to see how well people have got to know each other (it could be set up for use as 'a quick quiz'.) We find this type of activity works well on longer courses, and residential ones, where people have got to know each other a little better.

RAPPORT-BUILDING ICEBREAKERS

PLANE DAFT

Summary

Participants are hurried to make a paper plane, not quite knowing why, until it becomes clear that it was just a daft way of pairing them up!

Materials

Paper and marker pens.

Process

1. Split the room into two groups.
2. Ask one group to make paper planes, and quickly decorate them to reflect something of their personality.
3. Give each member of the other group a sheet of A4 paper and ask them to prepare a target which hints at what they like best in life.

Continued

Process (cont'd)

4. Give both groups one minute to do it. Tell them to write their first names somewhere on their work. Hurry them up!

5. Ask those with the targets to stand on one side of the room, with their targets face up at their feet.

6. Ask those with the planes to throw them from the other side of the room towards the targets.

7. Ask them to join up with the person whose target their plane landed closest to, for the paired interview.

What's the point?

This activity builds rapport in two ways:

- The group will all groan in unison when you reveal that all that hurrying up was for nothing more than to pair people up at random. Groaning in unison is rapport!

- The mood will now be light enough to make it almost unnecessary to ask them to discuss their artwork, which hints at their personalities. They will probably feel comfortable enough to ask each other anyway.

Variation

To link the activity to your course subject, ask them to hint at other (relevant) information about themselves. Eg, for an assertiveness course: on one wing of the plane they can draw a simple picture to illustrate how they generally deal with conflict, and on the other a number between one and ten to indicate how aware they are of the feelings of others. The target could reveal how good they are at getting their own way through picture/words.

Variation as a closer

Ask participants to throw the plane again. The person nearest to where it lands becomes their *buddy* for follow up after the course.

FOREHEAD

Summary
Participants move around the room asking questions about the information on other people's foreheads.

Materials
Post-it® notes and pens.

Process
1. Ask each participant to write two personal statements on a Post-it® note and stick it to their forehead.
2. Tell them to move around the room asking questions about other people's statements and answering questions about their own.

What's the point?
It is easier and less stressful to generate conversation when you have a point of focus (like asking about information on someone else's forehead) rather than being told to *go and meet each other*. It is also light-hearted and can set a relaxed tone for the day.

Variation

Specify subjects to write about rather than leaving it open, eg: two things about your schooldays, two things about your job, two things about your attitude, two things you would rather be doing than walking around with a Post-it® note stuck to your forehead.

Variation as a closer

Participants stick two action points to their foreheads, move around the room at high speed (possibly with Mission Impossible playing), and discuss their plans with their colleagues.

DICTIONARY

Summary
Participants use a random word as part of a self-introduction.

Materials
Dictionary.

Process

1. As part of the introductions, pass round a dictionary to each person in turn.
2. Tell them to open it at random and include the first word that they point to within their introduction.

What's the point?

Focusing on including a random word can take some of the fear out of introductions for people who are not used to talking in front of groups. The word provides the focus and it is fun.

Variation as a closer

Ask delegates to pick a word at random from the dictionary and find a way to *crowbar* that word into their closing comment for the day or their action plan comments.

MAGAZINE LIKE ME

Summary

Participants cut out a picture of a person from a magazine and introduce themselves, saying why they resemble the person they have chosen.

Materials

A pile of magazines, scissors, a cut-out of someone from a magazine, to whom you can draw some parallels from your own life.

Process

1. Set out your pile of magazines before everyone arrives.
2. During your own personal introduction, hold up a cut-out of someone from a magazine and say why you are like that person.
3. When you have finished (but before their introductions), refer the participants to the magazines you have set out. Invite them to spend three to four minutes scanning the magazines in order to cut out a picture of someone who reflects a part of their personality.

Process (cont'd)

4. Conduct your introductions in whatever way you decide (we recommend paired interview for this one) and add on the question: 'How are you like this person?'.

5. Participants hold up their magazine picture and draw whatever links they want to make between the person in the picture and themselves.

6. Ask the participants to stick the picture to their name cards, or somewhere visible to the rest of the group, where it will stay for the rest of the day.

What's the point?

This is a way of getting participants to say a little more about themselves than they normally might. The light-hearted feel to this type of 'party' introduction helps relax people and build trust and rapport more rapidly.

It also provides the trainer, as the day unfolds, with opportunities to refer back to anything said during the activity – whether it be a serious link to your content or a friendly comment to maintain an enjoyable atmosphere.

Variation

Ask the participants, pre-course, to bring a photo or other object which they can say reflects a part of their personality.

Variation as a closer

- Ask participants to pick a character they like from the magazines
- Ask them what this person would do in their situation, carrying out their action plan.
  Eg: 'I have chosen Clint Eastwood. He would not take any hassle and would face up to my scary boss with no self-doubt whatsoever.'

Bangs!

BANGS!

OPEN WITH IMPACT

The principle of the **bang**! is from John Townsend's *Trainer's Pocketbook*. He suggests you should do or say something in the first few minutes of the course to grab the listener's attention. The reason is that, on arrival, most participants are still thinking about their e-mails, their breakfast, their journey. The bang! brings them into the room, so that they are **mentally** as well as physically present.

Compare this to the lame, 'The toilets are in the hall, exits are over there, and here are the objectives…'. Boring! These things are important, but kill rapport if dealt with first **because** that is exactly what participants expect, and they won't really be listening.

Finishing with a bang! can also give your course a punchy and memorable finale, helping participants to leave with your main messages foremost in their minds.

The examples that follow are not necessarily revolutionary. You may well be familiar with the statistics quoted. The point is, bangs! work. They get people thinking about the course content straight away. Find out something really amazing, shocking, different or funny and include it in your opening preamble so that people sit up and think, 'Yes, maybe this person is worth listening to.'.

BANGS!

TOP TIPS FOR DELIVERY

- Bangs! tend to work better when they are linked to the course content. Examples include staggering statistics, stories, metaphors or anything out of the ordinary – see the examples on the following pages

- Deliver what you have to say in story-telling style or with impact. Help with this is available from http://www.thetrainingshop.co.uk who run story-telling workshops

- Project a bit of personality into doing this so that you sell it. This is important; in fact, most of our openers and closers need to be delivered with some gusto

- Use unashamed enthusiasm for delivering your messages. As John Townsend would say, 'If you are not enthusiastic, why should they be?' (*Trainer's Pocketbook*)

BANGS!

MEETINGS

Running successful meetings
Did you know that the average meeting costs around £amount to run? (*Work out figures by combining number of people by the average hour rate*). That is why, today, we are going to give you the techniques to make the most of those meetings.

For a bigger bang
Count out the money (monopoly money will do!) as you tell them these figures. Or fan it out, or dramatically stick it all, note by note, to a board (use spray-mount).

PRESENTATIONS

Presentation skills
In a classic survey it was found that people's number one fear was public speaking. Number three was death. Today, we will help you to reduce that fear.

For a bigger bang
Play the Death March music as you tell the statistic. Switch to something more lively as you say how today will help reduce that fear.

BANGS!

RISK

Risk management

Did you know that in 2003-2004, there were 235 fatal injuries to workers and prosecution by HSE was up 6% on the previous year? Don't let yourself become a statistic: this course will help to show you how. *(Source: HSE website)*

For a bigger bang

Lay out various items eg sock, kettle, brick, and ask which was the biggest killer in UK in 2004. Or ask which is the most/least dangerous occupation in terms of fatalities in 2004 and offer a list of ten to put in order. Or, if you are talking to administrative workers (where fatalities are lowest), and want to make a milder point, ask what is the biggest cause of time off in 2004. See http://www.hse.gov.uk/statistics for the answers and plenty more statistics to create openers relevant to your point.

Continued

BANGS!

ABSENCE

Managing absence

Did you know that in 2003, 2.2 million people suffered from work-related ill health? That is why it is important that absence is managed well to get people back to work as soon as possible. This course will help to show you how.

For a bigger bang

Ask the participants to discover the number of days (estimated) to have been lost within their teams through absence. Add them all together and tally the approximate cost of the absence.

CUSTOMER CARE

Bad news travels fast...

Did you know that when people are unhappy with the service they receive from you, they are likely to tell 10-12 other people? The good news is that some of the messages from this course will help to turn your customers around with ease.

For a bigger bang

As a visual back up: have an enormous pile of complaint letters sitting next to a tiny pile of thanking letters! (Use blank A4 with just one of each kind on top!)

TONE SETTERS USING METAPHOR, ANALOGY & DIALOGUE

TONE SETTERS

MEMORABLE OPENINGS

Tone setters are short statements that engage the senses. You introduce the subject by using a link to something that the delegates already know. We have some examples in this section, and we encourage you to use your own. When you get it right, you will often hear delegates say, at the end, that the most memorable thing about the course was the analogy that you used at the beginning!

This response has made us think hard about why using opening tone setters is so effective, and we think these are the reasons why they stand out so much:

- People's attention is highest at the beginning of an event (primacy effect, in psychological talk)

- We instantly relate to and are more prepared to learn about new subjects, if a link can be made, early on, to the similar principles of something we already know

- Stories create mental images, which are stored in our long-term memory

TONE SETTERS

MEMORABLE OPENINGS

Why tone setters are effective (cont'd)

- Stories we can relate to engage the emotional part of the brain, which causes us to become involved (we can't help it!)

- Tone setters provide an anchor for the rest of the detail that follows, and so can be referred back to throughout the day to provide a *bird's eye* view of the whole point, when people are getting lost in the detail

- Or perhaps it is just that Alan and Paul are only exciting for about ten minutes a day!

Anyway, here are a few examples for you to try. We find these are even more powerful if you back them up with a picture or an object that is linked to the theme.
(We have included relevant picture suggestions.)

1. LISTENING AND QUESTIONING SKILLS

Don't get in a rut

Say something like, 'Regular practice of good questioning and listening skills is like creating deeper and deeper ruts on a muddy lane. The deeper the ruts, the more noticeable it is when you 'bump' out of them.'

'The link to today's course is that the more practice you have of using these skills, the more you will create those deep ruts and notice when you bump out of them and start interrupting, or using any other bad communication habits.'

Picture suggestion ▶ A muddy lane (from a catalogue or magazine)

2. MEETINGS

Carry on Doctor

Say something like, 'When you last went to visit your GP, were you prepared to walk away without answers to your questions, some idea of a future outcome or at least some tangible result?   The answer is probably no. Well, why would you go into a meeting without the same expectation? Today's course is going to give you some top tips on how to get the most from your meetings.'

Picture suggestion ▶ A prescription – preferably photocopied to A3 so everyone can see it.

45

3. MANAGER SKILLS

It's good to talk

Say something like, 'People tend to go to the Samaritans when things get really bad. The Samaritans' job is to listen without judgment. So, when things are really bad, the best thing to do is to listen without judgment. Question: why wait for things to get so bad before you do this. Today's course is about helping you to listen without judgment, which will be very useful when you are coaching or mentoring or even during a disciplinary interview.'

Variation

Ask, 'What are the skills and attitude of the Samaritans?'. 'Which ones are relevant to you as a manager and which ones are not?' (This could be done in a large group led by you, or in smaller groups to lead to a discussion.)

Picture suggestion ▶ The Samaritans' logo or telephone number

4. CUSTOMER CARE

Public praise

Say something like, 'If you think now about the last time someone really praised you and also the last time someone criticized you, which one comes more easily to mind? Which type do you have more examples of? We tend to remember negative things more readily than positives. This is the same for people who work with the public; it can be easy to forget that we do in fact like people; we can let the negative experiences dominate. Now unless you work in the complaints department, I suggest to you that when dealing with the public, there is at least a 50/50 split between good and bad experiences. The positive may even outweigh the negative. It is very easy to lump all the experiences together, both good and bad, into pure negativity. Today's course will give you the skills to deal with the negative elements of working with the public in a way that allows you to take a more balanced view.'

Picture suggestion ▶ Person crying or laughing or the Theatre happy/sad symbol

5. FEEDBACK

Pants

Say something like, 'I would like to tell you a story about some pants. When I was seven, I received a present from my aunt. It was beautifully wrapped and I couldn't wait to see what was inside. As I tore it open, I was suddenly disappointed to see what it was – a very large pair of underpants that would not even fit an average-sized adult. It was not what I was hoping for; I had no use for them whatsoever. Eventually, we decided to cut them up and use them as house dusters.'

'Feedback is exactly the same. The process of giving feedback is like giving someone a gift. You need to wrap it up as well as you can so that it is as acceptable to the receiver. The recipient will have a mixture of feelings about what they are about to receive. They may be looking forward to it or dreading it. When they do get it, it may not be what they wanted. The point is that they have a choice whether they think the feedback is good, can be used or not; whether to accept it or whether they just decide it is pants! Today's course will help you to put feedback together that is useful and as acceptable as it can be to others.'

Picture suggestion ▶ Wrapped up pants (draw it yourself or bring in the real thing!)

6. COACHING

Garlic & Baked Beans

Say something like, 'When you are trying to help people raise their awareness of their actions, perhaps through coaching, there are two types of people: Garlic people and Baked Bean people. If you consume large amounts of either foodstuff you will have an impact upon others!'

'Most often, when you eat a lot of garlic everyone else is aware of the impact whilst you are not. When you consume large amounts of baked beans, we are all aware of the impact. And so it is with people: some act in a way that shows they are not aware of the impact their behaviour has upon others: they are Garlic people. Those who are very aware of their impact are Baked Bean types. Is it fair to say that giving coaching or feedback to these two types should be different depending on how aware they are of their own impact?'

'Today's course will help you to adapt your style to these different types of people.'

Picture suggestion ▶ Some garlic and a can of baked beans

7. CUSTOMER CARE

A good buffing

At the beginning of the course, as you are about to introduce yourself, ask for a volunteer to come up (choose someone who is wearing black shoes). As you introduce yourself, and without interrupting what you are saying (you need to be able to multi-task), polish their shoes in old shoeshine style. Do not make any reference to what you are doing. When you have finished, ask the volunteer to return to their seat. Ask the participants, 'What was the point of that?'.

Some answers that you might like to build on are that you were doing more than they would have expected, which is part of what customer care is all about. Do not accept any money from the participant!

8. FEEDBACK

Good Dog

Say something like, 'When you praise your dog for doing its business in your back garden you would never say, *Well done, Fido, for using the correct part of the garden to toilet in, I am very pleased with your behaviour, thank you.* You would just say, *Good boy*. No reason to say anything else.'

'By the same token, it is **not** appropriate just to say *well done* or the equivalent of *good boy*, without saying why, to adults. Adults need praise to be conditional, ie linked to something that they have done. Eg: *Thanks for getting that report done so quickly; it really helped me when I had to present it to the board.*'

'So, in summary, don't praise humans as if they were dogs.'

 Dog biscuits

51

9. PRESENTING INFORMATION

Washing machine

Say something like, 'When you have information to convey to people, it is a bit like when you put your washing on. You want to cram everything into the machine but you know that if you do, it won't get covered in water properly. You therefore put less in so that it gets done properly. The same is true of putting information across to people. You need to think to yourself: what is the optimum amount to communicate to make sure I do not overload and everything is covered properly?

This course will help you to prioritise the important messages to put across.'

Picture suggestion ▶ Packet of washing powder

10. PUBLIC SPEAKING/PRESENTING

Loft extension

Say something like, 'When you are about to speak in public it is useful to think of a loft extension. If you are fortunate enough to get your loft extended, you can expand your house by up to about 30%. If someone were to ask you if that loft was still part of your house, you would say yes.

It is the same when you come to speak in public. You are just extending yourself by 30% but you are still being yourself; it is still you. Sometimes people hold back when they speak as they forget the 30% rule. If you don't increase your presence by 30%, you will not be seen! Today's course will give you the tips on how to extend yourself by 30% without losing your steady foundations.'

11. COACHING

Seat belt

Say something like, 'I was in a friend's car while we did the school run with his children. One of his children is four years old and is trying to learn to do up her own seat belt. I watched as she struggled to put it on. I was about to help, when my friend sensed this and stopped me. His daughter took another two minutes but was eventually successful. When I asked him afterwards why he let her struggle so, especially as we were running late, he told me that she had to learn sometime and it did not make it okay to rob her of that, just because we were under time pressure.'

'This is exactly what coaching is like. Part of your role as a coach/manager is to let people struggle a bit so that they can learn on their own. It is particularly important, when work is so busy, to remind yourself that if you don't allow time now for them to learn, will any other time really be that much better? Today's course will help with some of those common coaching dilemmas.'

Picture suggestion ▶ Seat belt

FILTERS

FILTERS

INTRODUCTION

The idea of opening filters works on the NLP principle that we take in information that is linked to what we want to know about, or are programmed to listen for. One simple example is your name: you can usually hear that spoken at some distance away even when you can't hear the rest of the conversation.

So, if you give people elements of the course information early on, you help them to set up some filters in their heads to listen out for the content that most interests them.

...mumble mumble
RUPERT mumble...

DRINKS N CARDS

Summary
Participants learn about the course by reading what's written on their *coffee mat*.

Materials
Pieces of card.

Process
1. Place a card with some information about the course under participants' coffee cups or put it under each person's chair at the beginning of the day.
2. Ask them to talk to one another about what they have found out (this probably works best after the initial introductions).

What's the point?
Pre-reviewing the course like this will cause participants both to generate interest for the subject(s) and to *filter in* the information as you deliver it, since it will all relate to the discussions, directed by your cards, that they had earlier in the morning.

GROUND RULES PLEDGE

Summary

Participants agree on behaviours they do and don't want from each other within the session.

Materials

Flipchart paper, pens, musical instruments (optional).

Process

1. Split the delegates into two or three groups.
2. Their job is to establish their own ground rules – a guide for the way they want to work together to get the best out of the day. (Say: 'The purpose of establishing ground rules is to prevent behaviour that you don't want, and encourage behaviour that you do want, from each other and from me. As a starting point, consider courses or events you have attended in the past and think of all the good and not so good things that happened. Now generate rules to encourage more of the good and less of the not so good.')

Process (cont'd)

3. Tell participants to come up with some ground rules for their own group.
   However, they need to find a way to make these rules memorable.
   For example, by presenting them as a song, rhyme, poem, picture or story, etc.
4. The only rule is that the rules should be **clear** and **memorable**.
5. Give them 20 minutes.
6. Reconvene after the time has elapsed and ask each group in turn to reveal their ground rules in their chosen way.
7. As each group concludes, ask the other groups if they agree with the proposed rules, and if so to sign up to them.
8. Remind the whole group that your job as trainer/facilitator is to keep the group to these rules.

What's the point?

It is important to establish clear boundaries early on in the course. Agreed ground rules are sometimes so wishy-washy that they are not bought into by delegates and end up being a waste of time. No one can keep to rules they are unsure of! This exercise is fun and the rules are clear **and** memorable.

HUNT FOR LEARNING

Summary
Participants pre-review course material by identifying objects of interest, linked to the session which will follow, to include in their introductions to each other.

Materials
See step 1.

Process
1. Set up your room as you normally would for a high quality learning session, including as a minimum:
   - Welcome poster
   - Posters around the room which relate to the course concepts
   - Interesting and colourful workbooks
   - Props
   - Handouts, etc

Process (cont'd)

2. Introduce yourself and the course.
3. Invite the participants to search the room, identify one item or concept which catches their interest and find out more about it, ready to include in their introduction for the day.
4. Allow the participants the freedom of the room, ie if they want to look **now** at the handouts that you will be giving out later on, to find an item of interest, let them!
5. Ask them to include what they have found out about their item as part of their introductions to each other.

What's the point?

Pre-reviewing the course like this makes participants generate interest in the subject(s). They will also *filter* in the information as you deliver it later in the day, since it will all relate to the items they discussed earlier.

Variation as a closer

Ask them to tell you what was the one object of interest that stood out from today's course and why.

NOTES

SUBJECT OPENERS

INTRODUCTION

This section contains what we have called 'Subject Openers' and they are similar in style to the activities in our first book: *Icebreakers Pocketbook*. The idea behind these exercises is to engage people's brains in the content of the course whilst they are also getting to know each other.

The activities tend to work best if **linked** to course content rather than being too general. We have found time and time again that the more linked the opening activity is to the content or even the style of the course, the better the results you get from the event itself.

ASSERTIVENESS

FOUR ANIMALS

Aim
To make memorable the four behaviours which are linked to assertiveness.

Learning
Identify the typical behaviours of each of the four styles. Identify one of four animals you find most closely represents the way you are viewed/feel/behave.

Materials
Toy owl, bull, sheep and fox (or snake). Sheet of flipchart paper.

Four cards reading:

I'm OK, You're OK.	I'm OK, You're not OK.
I'm not OK, You're OK.	I'm not OK, You're not OK.

Trainer knowledge needed

Working knowledge of the theory of assertiveness.
Some understanding of animal characters as used in children's stories would
be helpful but not essential!

Process

1. Introduce the subject of assertiveness including passiveness, aggressiveness
   and passive-aggressiveness.
2. Draw a cross to make a matrix on a piece of flipchart paper and place it on the
   floor/table. Place the four animals on the flipchart paper, one in each box.
3. Split the group into four and allocate each group an animal from the matrix.
   Ask each group to identify the stereotypical characteristics of their animal (as may
   be told in a children's story). Which of the four assertiveness behaviours do they
   think each animal relates to?
4. Hand out the four cards reading: *I'm OK, you're not OK* etc and ask them to place
   each card inside the matrix with the animal they believe it relates to.

Process (cont'd)
5. They will eventually have:

I'm OK,
You're OK.

Owl – Assertive. Avoids instinctive behaviours, remains calm, looks at facts, makes informed choices, responds rather than reacts

I'm OK,
You're not OK.

Bull – Aggressive. Instinctively fights when confronted, believing fight to be the best method of self-preservation. No apparent concern for others. Hot headed, emotional, reacts rather than responds

I'm not OK,
You're OK.

Sheep – Passive. Instinctively runs when confronted, believing flight to be the best method of self-preservation. No apparent concern for self. Quiet, timid, amenable, reacts rather than responds

Process (cont'd)

| I'm not OK, You're not OK. |

Fox/Snake – Passive-Aggressive. Instinctively runs when confronted, believing they cannot win any direct confrontation. However, has as little respect for others as for self. May not have the self-esteem to stand up for their own rights (like the sheep) but also wants to bypass your rights (like the bull). Does this indirectly and can often be found whispering their frustrations under their breath, or to anyone but the person they should be speaking to about their issues.

What's the point?

This activity should be used as a tool for facilitating a conversation, rather than in any sort of presentation. It is designed to instigate sharing of opinions.

Variation as a closer

Use the four animals when you review the day.

ASSERTIVENESS

PLAYDOUGH FEELINGS

Aim

To create dialogue and promote thinking about how feelings change from moment to moment, and how these changes impact on our ability to be assertive.

Learning

Participants will reflect their feelings in a model they create, which they will then explain.

Materials

Playdough.
Blank name cards.

Process

1. Give each participant a lump of playdough.
2. Ask them to consider how they feel right now, and to mould the model into a shape that reflects this.
3. Hand out a 5" x 3" card to each person and ask them to name it.

Process (cont'd)

4. Ask each participant in turn to bring their model and card over to a *display* table (where the models will sit for the day), and on the way to give a 30-second talk explaining what feelings the model represents.
5. After each participant has explained their model and placed it on the table, emphasize the fact that, thanks to the models, we now have in the room an overt and visual overview of everyone's feelings, something we often make assumptions about.
6. Leave the models on the table and use them to draw light-hearted links throughout the day between the behaviour of your participants and their models.

What's the point?

Assertiveness is about using behaviour as a clue to the feelings of others, giving us the opportunity to ask good quality questions to check our thinking against the facts. Anyone on your course who is new to assertiveness training may think of it as *deep* and *heavy*. This opener will help to make the point early and keep the link between behaviour and feelings simple and alive throughout the day – and fun!

Variation
(*Or in addition*) Hand each participant a bendy man (available from www.thetrainingshop.co.uk) and ask them to bend its limbs into body language which reflects their feelings at that moment. Ask them to continue with this activity throughout the day: each time they realise that their mood has changed, bend the man and hold it up. Keep it very light-hearted. Give prizes (sweets) or lavish praise to those who do so. More reluctant participants will soon follow if it feels safe and fun.

Variation as a closer
Ask participants to model how they feel about the day or the course, or what they know or will do, using the playdough. Review individually as a light-hearted way to end.

TEAMS

SHAPES

Aim
Generate interest in the subject of high-performing teams.

Learning
Link the results of a teambuilding activity to the benefits of having a diverse team.

Materials
Eight tennis balls (or any uniform shapes). Eight shapes/objects including a triangle, a square, a blob of slime, a ball of stretchy putty and anything with an unusual texture which might make people say they don't like its touch, smell or look. The pocket money sections of toy shops have all sorts of strange things!)

Process
1. Divide your group into two teams.
2. Give one team the eight tennis balls (or anything else that is a uniform shape, eg eight square blocks).
3. Give the other team the varied eight items.
4. Ask them both to create something that will be interesting for the other team to look at, using only the items they have been given.
5. Give them five minutes to create.

What's the point?
When they have completed their creations, ask them to compare them. Generally, the group with the varied objects have more choices open to them and so they usually create a more interesting result.
(The point being that variety brings more choices and more scope for difference.)

In teams, it is easy to recruit and be drawn to people similar to ourselves, but more is possible if you have a varied range of people.

Variation as a closer
Do exactly the same, but at the end of the day!

NEW MANAGER

BOOKLETS

Aim
To move new managers, supervisors and team leaders away from **doing** the job to **managing others** who are doing the job.

Learning
Participants will discuss how *letting go* (of power) makes them feel, list the benefits of empowering others, and plan a personal strategy to move from being responsible for the task to being accountable for the results.

Materials
Flipchart with pre-prepared sheet.
A course booklet per participant.

Process

1. After your welcome and initial introductions to the course and materials, give each participant a booklet and use the paired interview technique to get them talking to each other. For example, give participants 15 minutes to interview each other using the format below, which you should pre-write on a flipchart:
   - Name and role
   - What is your experience of being managed?
   - What is your experience of managing others?
   - What is your favourite management moment (good or bad, personal or famous)?
   - If you could only get one thing out of being here today, what would it be?

2. Call time at 15 minutes. Ask each participant to take their partner's booklet, pick a page and capture all that they remember about them from the interview in any way they see fit. The only caveat is that it must be memorable. Then, before they hand the booklet back, ask them to introduce their partners to the rest of the group, using the information they have discovered.

Process (cont'd)

3. At the end of each introduction ask the interviewer to pass the booklet back to its owner.

4. Ask the owner how they feel about having someone else capture information about them, in their booklet, and introduce them to the group?

5. How well do they think the information was captured and relayed?

6. Could they have done better themselves?

7. After all interviews have taken place, draw the link to a difficulty faced by many new managers. A new manager must move away from *doing the job themselves* to watching others doing it (differently, better, worse, slower, quicker), as they begin to learn the skills of management, eg planning, directing, organising and controlling.

8. Discuss in plenary:

   ● What are the benefits of handing over power to others to do a job?

   ● Do these outweigh the drawbacks?

   ● What difficulties / obstacles do you anticipate in doing this?

   ● How will you overcome them?

What's the point?
Many new managers have been promoted from within the team. This activity is particular, though not exclusive, to their predicament. It helps put into context the fact that moving into a position of managing people or a team requires a particular set of skills, often very different from the one being used by the team, whose skills will relate to the completion of tasks which contribute to the overall result.

Variation as a closer
Ask participants to discuss an action plan that they intend to implement as a consequence of their learning from the course. Then get them to swap booklets.
Ask each participant to capture their partner's action plan in their partner's booklet.
Draw the links as above.

TIME MANAGEMENT

LISTS

Aim
To encourage internal questioning of *how I use my time*.

Learning
Participants will identify the part they play in preventing their time from *being eaten*.

Materials
Pre-prepared flipchart sheet.

Process

1. After all introductions have been made and you have gained rapport with the group, split the delegates into three groups for your first activity of the day.
2. Tell each group to discover (from your list on a pre-prepared flipchart) which member of the group:
   a. Has been to the most places in the world
   b. Owns an antique
   c. Knows an Aborigine
   d. Has a link to Russia
   e. Feels bored
   f. Has ever owned a cup with their name on it
   g. Has ever worn a Christmas jumper
   h. Has done a runner from a restaurant
   i. Was ever 'caned' at school
   j. Had/has a friend called Harry

Process (cont'd)

3. Do not allocate a time for this activity.
4. Allow people to enjoy themselves for as long as they like (within reason: 15 minutes at most). Then call time.
5. Ask: 'How do you feel about that as an activity? What did you get from it? What was the point? How does the activity relate to the subject of time management? Why did you engage in it?'
6. The group's answers to these questions should provide you with all the links you need and will make the point for you. If not, see **What's the point?** on the next page and make the links yourself.

What's the point?

You cannot manipulate time, you just have it. It is there for your use (or misuse). Failure, poverty, unhappiness and lack of self-awareness need no plan to be found; we may freely stumble upon any of them. However, success, riches, happiness and self-awareness can be gained with the help of a good plan. A good plan for the way we use our time.

This activity emphasizes how easy it can be to be sidetracked. We do not always exercise our powers of discrimination. One of the many pillars of good time management is that we should think about and evaluate potential activities, and ask ourselves: 'how does this fit in with my goals and objectives?'.

Variation

Use any pointless activity that clearly has no relation to the goals of anyone in the room.

PRESENTATION SKILLS

LAUNDROMAT

Aim
To put the theory of *presenting* into perspective.

Learning
Use an analogy to assess presentation skills.

Materials
None.

Process

1. At some point early on in your presentations course use the following analogy to put presentation skills into perspective:
   When people walk into a presentation, they are offering the presenter their minds, for the period of the presentation, to work their presentation magic on. It is a little like offering your clothes to a Laundromat worker. The presenter is the person doing the washing:
   - You can put too many clothes in.
   - You can put the temperature up too high or too low.
   - You can add too much or too little washing powder
   - You can time the wash to be too long or too short
   - You can mix clothes of different colours

Process (cont'd)

2. Draw the links:
   - Including too much information
   - Being over-enthusiastic or too deadpan
   - Over-using media like PowerPoint or video
   - Timing your presentation all wrong
   - Misjudging your audience

However, if you know your job
(*have read the label*) and follow
the basic rules, the clothes
will emerge exactly as
you intended.

What's the point?

The story helps to put presenting into a frame which everyone can relate to.
You can use it to keep reviews and feedback from any mini-presentations during
your course simple, comprehensible and fun. You can ask questions like:

- If we, your audience, were clothes how would you describe our condition now that
  your presentation (*washing cycle*) is at an end?
- If there was a label on us (*advice for washing clothes*) what would it say?
- With reference to the positive parts of their presentations: What did you do/say to
  cause that to happen? (*Got the temperature right / timed it right / didn't include too
  much, etc*)

Variation

Get the participants to draw the links themselves. Anything goes: there isn't a right or
wrong answer.

PRESENTATION SKILLS

ABCD

Aim
To start a presentation with confidence.

Learning
Use an ABCD format to introduce yourself.
Use an ABCD format to begin a presentation.

Materials
Pre-written flipchart with:
A. *Tell us an amazing fact about yourself.*
B. *What do you hope to get from this course?*
C. *How would you rate yourself out of 10 as a presenter and why?*
D. *How and when do you intend to put your new-found skills into practice after today?*

Process

1. At the beginning of your course ask participants to introduce themselves to the group, using the format you have pre-written on the flipchart.

2. Once all the introductions have been made, smugly point out that they have all just used a technique that many famous presenters use to begin a presentation. Namely:

   A – Attention   (get the attention of your audience)
   B – Benefits   (tell them what they will get from listening to you)
   C – Credentials   (sell yourself – why should your audience listen to you?)
   D – Direction   (make the intended journey for your presentation clear – audiences don't like surprises!)

3. Say something like: 'The only difference is that you have used the technique reflectively, to introduce yourself rather than to make a presentation. The principle is the same.'

What's the point?

ABCD is so easy to remember that it brings confidence even for impromptu presentations. This activity gets people using the format and feeling the confidence it gives. This format can be used to form the *beginning* of any presentation. (It is generally followed by the *body* then the *conclusion*.)

Variation

Introduce yourself using this process and ask the participants if they can spot any pattern to what you said, or familiar techniques used. If not, reveal how you remembered what to say by using ABCD.

COACHING

TRACK N FIELD

Aim
To help put coaching into context by putting learners in the shoes of the coachee.

Learning
Discuss the merits of playing to the strengths of the coachee.

Materials
Paper and pens.

Trainer knowledge needed
A basic knowledge of the principles of business coaching.

Process
1. Hand out a piece of paper to each participant.
   Ask everyone to write down a school sport or activity which they were particularly good at or enjoyed.
2. Collect all the papers back in.
3. Hand them out at random to each participant making sure that no one receives their own.
4. Pair the participants up. Ask them to coach each other to help them become better at the subject on their sheet.

What's the point?

You can't coach anyone if they don't have the will to do the job!
Coaching is a great management tool to help people to maximise their
potential to do a task or achieve a goal of their own choosing.
To be able to use the skills of coaching effectively the coachee
must have some willingness to want to succeed, and some
skills in the area in which they are being coached.

In short – coach people in areas in which **they** wish
to excel not in which **you** wish them to excel.
Spend more time playing to their
strengths rather than trying to
fix their weaknesses.

WOGGLE SNATCHING

COACHING OR QUESTIONING SKILLS

80/20

Aim
To help participants learn the difference between asking and telling.

Learning
What the 80/20 ratio actually feels like.

Materials
Enough stopwatches for the group to work in trios.

Process

1. Begin a coaching session or practice session for questioning skills in trios.
2. Allocate the roles of coach, coachee and observer.
3. On every occasion that the coach speaks, the observer records the length of time and makes a note of the total time that the coach talked for.
4. When practice has finished, divide the total time of the session by the amount of time the coach was talking; this will give you a rough percentage of time that the coach was talking.
5. Tell them that the aim is to get as close as possible to 20% talking time for the coach.

What's the point?
This activity makes participants focus on exactly how long they are talking for, and what listening for 80% of the time **really** feels like.

Variation
Use this for facilitation skills courses to time how much intervention the facilitator makes.

Variation as a closer
This can be used as a final test for participants, or indeed at any point during the whole day.

COMMUNICATION SKILLS

ASK A SILLY QUESTION

Aim
Participants test their understanding of a range of question types.

Learning
Identify and ask different types of question.

Materials
List of question types (as prompts for the trainer). Pre-prepared sets of ten stepping stones (paper will do!).

Process

1. At the end of the training session split your group into two teams.

2. Lay out two sets of ten stepping-stones, stretching from one side of the room to the other. The object of the game is to be the team who gets one of their members across the room, via the stepping-stones, by generating questions of a specific type to ask the other team.

3. The trainer runs this by calling out instructions, eg 'Team A: I want you to ask Team B an open question – linked to the course.'

4. If Team A use the right type of question, they move forward one space. Team B stay where they are – for now!

Process (cont'd)
5. Then the teams swap.
6. You now ask Team B to come up with a different type of question for Team A, eg a hypothetical one, linked to the course. If they ask the question to your satisfaction, they move forward one space.

Types of question
Ask team 'x' a **multiple** question
Ask team 'x' an **open** question
Ask team 'x' a **closed** question
Ask team 'x' a **probing** question
Ask team 'x' a **focused** question
Ask team 'x' a **reflecting** question

Ask team 'x' a **hypothetical** question
Ask team 'x' a **rhetorical** question
Ask team 'x' a **clarifying** question
Ask team 'x' a **leading** question
Ask team 'x' a **stupid** question

What's the point?
Review course content by practising using questions.

Variation as a closer
The trainer could ask questions about the course, or set tasks for each team, instead of asking for questions from the team.

DIVERSITY

PHOTOFIT

Aim
To identify common images in the media and discuss them.

Learning
What is acceptable and what is not.

Materials
A mix of magazines (*for best effect choose a mixture of magazines designed specifically for men, women, ethnic minorities, teenagers, and other specific groups*).
A glue stick, several pairs of scissors, flipchart.

Process
1. Split your group into three teams and hand each team a pile of magazines.
2. Ask delegates to find pictures of people doing things, cut them out and stick them onto a piece of flipchart paper.
3. Ask them to look at the images and answer the questions:
   - In what way are people portrayed in these magazines?
   - What are your thoughts as you look at the people in the pictures?
   - What would they be good at?
   - Who would you trust? Who do you like least? Why? Who is your favourite? Why?
   - Are they fair images?
4. Allow a discussion.

What's the point?
It is easy to accept blindly what is portrayed in the media. It goes without saying it is wrong – but that is the problem, it does go without saying. This session is designed to raise awareness of all the potentially offensive images that can be found. On the flipside, it also allows people to identify *where the line is* so that they become more aware of when they may have crossed it and caused offence.

Variation/extra questions
- Do the images show people fairly?
- Is anyone stereotyped?
- Are men/women shown favouring particular occupations?
- What about images of people who are disabled, gay, of different ethnic origins?
- What is the agenda of the advert or magazine it came from?

Variation as a closer
Follow the same format with an extra closing comment: 'As you prepare to re-join the real world, take a look at this freely available literature. I would like to hear your comments.'

TRAIN THE TRAINER

WELCOME

Aim

To generate a positive atmosphere in the training room.

Learning

Compare course participants to personal house guests and generate tips for creating a welcoming atmosphere.

Materials

Flipchart and pens.

Process

1. On a flipchart, write the following, 'What are the key things that you do to welcome guests to your house? What do you do in advance and what do you do when they arrive?'.

2. Ask participants for their answers and, using their words, list replies on the flipchart.

3. Next, tack up the sheet to make it visible and on the next sheet of flipchart paper write at the top: 'What do we do to welcome people to our courses?'

4. Ask the group to link the first set of suggestions to the second one to create a list. Eg, if someone suggests, 'Phone beforehand with directions', you can ask, 'How does this relate to courses?' Answers might include, 'I would make sure that I send out really good joining instructions'.

What's the point?

New trainers can be nervous and so naturally become self-concerned at the start of a course. Experienced trainers can easily forget how nervous, indifferent, keen, bored, etc participants can be when arriving for a course. This activity will get the participants thinking about their future delegates and what they need to do to make them feel welcome.

Variation

Ask the group what the point was of including such a question and generating a list of advice from it. They will hopefully make the connections themselves.

Variation as a closer

Ask them to think about what they are going to do, as a result of this course, to look after their participants.

TRAIN THE TRAINER

JUGGLER

Aim
Bring the concept of attitude, skills and knowledge to life.

Learning
This is a chance to rate your attitude, skills and knowledge as a trainer, using juggling. You do not need to be able to juggle.

Materials
Juggling balls, flipchart sheets, marker pens.

Process
1. Pin up three flipchart sheets with 'Attitude' 'Skills' and 'Knowledge' written on each one respectively. Draw a line on each from the top right-hand corner (write 'High' here) to the bottom left-hand corner (write 'Low' here). Ask delegates to come up and indicate with a marker how they would rate themselves as trainers in terms of: their **attitude** towards helping others learn, their **knowledge** of how others learn best and their **skill** level at actually helping others learn.
2. Ask for a volunteer. Hold up the juggling balls and explain for the group to hear that you would like to learn to juggle – but, alas, haven't until this point found a reputable trainer. Ask the volunteer to help you to learn to juggle for the next three minutes!

Process (cont'd)

3. Do exactly as you are told, answer the questions that are put to you and generally be a good student for the next three minutes.
4. After the time has elapsed get the group to give the volunteer a round of applause. Ask the volunteer and then the group what they did that was good in terms of helping you to learn. Draw links between their answers and good training / facilitating / coaching practice.
5. Ask the volunteer to revisit the three flipcharts and, on reflection, change any of their personal ratings. Ask the rest of the group to do the same (note: the volunteer may legitimately change all three but the group should not change skills as sitting passively does not enhance skill, though it may change attitudes or improve knowledge).

What's the point?

This activity provides links to subjects you may be covering in your Train the Trainer course including: feedback, learning styles, learning cycle, evaluating training effectiveness, trainer delivery styles and methods, and more.

QUALITY

THAT TAKES THE BISCUIT

Aim
To put across the importance of quality and continuous improvement.

Learning
Quality is everywhere.

Materials
Packet of HobNobs, tin

Process
1. Dramatically open a packet of chocolate HobNobs in front of everyone and pour the biscuits into a tin.
2. Walk around offering a biscuit to each participant (ask them not to eat it yet).
3. Tell them to hold up the biscuits and then ask: 'Do they all look the same? Take a bite – does it taste the same as chocolate Hobnobs you have had before? Did you expect it to taste the same?'
4. Make the point that every type of biscuit, in every packet, on every shelf in every shop in the country and the world should!! This demonstrates the importance of quality – how does it relate to us today?

What's the point?
It brings the subject of quality rapidly down to earth where people can relate to it.

Variation
Erm...use Garibaldis or custard creams!

Variation as a closer
Use the same activity as a punchy review to leave them with for the end of day.

LISTENING SKILLS

MUSIC TO MY EARS

Aim
Focused listening.

Learning
Relate the skills used when listening to music to the skills used when listening to people.

Materials
Stereo.
Music (suggest *Ghost Town* by The Specials or *Let it be* by The Beatles – basically you need to choose something fairly well known and with more than one instrument in)

Trainer knowledge needed:
Active/global listening skills.

Process
1. Prepare to play a piece of music.
2. Create the same number of groups as there are instruments in the piece.
3. Give each group an instrument to focus on.
4. Ask them to listen **only** to their allocated instrument and note what the instrument is doing.
5. After the piece is finished ask them to describe what the music was doing as a whole.

What's the point?
The point is that if you want to practise your listening skills, part of the technique is to remove all other distractions apart from the one thing that you are listening to. When focusing on just the base line of a piece of lively pop music, it is difficult not to be distracted by what the other instruments are doing.

BELBIN TEAM ROLES

LET'S GO FOR A WALK

Aim
To make Belbin team roles and traits memorable to your course participants.

Learning
Match the characters from a story to each of the Belbin team roles.

Materials
Two sets of nine cards with brief overviews of the traits of each Belbin team role.
The story overleaf.

Trainer knowledge needed:
Basic knowledge of the Belbin team roles.

Process
1. Tell the story (overleaf) with gusto!
2. Split the group into two and hand out a full set of cards to each.
3. Ask them to try to match the characters in the story to the traits of each team role.

Process (cont'd)

4. Debrief answers (keeping it light-hearted as the learning comes from searching for the links rather than getting it right).
5. Explain to the group that you would like to tell them a bizarre story which will provide a mental link for the session and will alleviate the need for constant reference to notes to check details about the Belbin team roles. Tell the participants that, in the story, they will go to three locations (their office, their local gym and their local pub) and will meet three characters in each location.

Office

(Plant)

Here you meet a man who resembles Einstein, with wild hair and a long white coat. He is over at the window gazing up into the clouds and is deep in thought. You call to him but he doesn't hear. Just then he clicks his fingers and a light bulb appears above his head as he says, 'I have it!'

(Monitor evaluator)
In another part of your office is a man in a long black gown, wearing what looks like a judge's wig. He is drinking a can of non-alcoholic lager. He is standing quite still while taking stock of all of the information in the office, occasionally murmuring '*hmmm*'.

(Specialist)
Sitting down at a desk is a woman engrossed in a book. It is a very rare book – only three copies of it exist. It is the size of an enormous encyclopedia, which appears to sparkle. It may hold the keys to the universe. When you attempt to talk to the woman she appears uninterested in anything you have to say – until you ask her about the book and its contents. Then she comes alive with conversation, which you find hard to follow.

Pub

(Co-ordinator)

As you enter your local pub a tall, mature chap with slicked back hair, dressed in the kind of attire you would expect a music conductor to wear, welcomes you with a confident tone and waves you towards the other two people at the table. You join them.

(Team-worker)

At the table is a mousy looking character with huge ears, drinking a pint of mild. She is listening with great empathy and speaking softly to another person. She shares her knowledge of the little known talents available within her team.

(Resource investigator)

The third person has been interrupted by a call on her enormous mobile phone and is talking on it with great enthusiasm. She eagerly asks many questions and takes notes of the answers. She asks the caller to hold while she takes another incoming call and handles it with the same smoothness.

Gym

(Shaper)
As you approach the gym you hear bellowing and soon realise it is directed at you.
A large chap, looking like a circus ringmaster from a children's book, with top hat, red
jacket, white trousers, black boots and a whip, is looking at his watch. He says to you,
'Come along, you should have been here an hour ago', and cracks his whip, making you
speed up as you enter the gym.

(Implementer)
Inside is a well-built man with a no-nonsense look about him. His sleeves are rolled up
and with one hand he is turning a cog, which in turn rotates several other cogs. In his
other hand is a huge piece of paper, headed 'Objectives'. Each time the man makes a
turn of the cog he ticks off a line on the page with a satisfied air. He is sweating but
looks too focused to consider stopping.

(Completer/finisher)
Moving slowly around the room is a woman holding a gigantic magnifying glass. She
uses it to scan every detail of the gym's equipment to ensure that everything is in good
working order. She looks anxious and frequently asks the cog turner to stop, while she
brushes away a speck of dust or pulls out a hair, much to his irritation.

What's the point?

This is a memorable story to commit to participants' minds the traits of the Belbin team roles. It uses a journey linked to familiar places, imagery and metaphor to help recall the traits, eg:

Office
- Plant – Einstein, deep in thought, light bulb
- Monitor evaluator – judge's wig, non-alcoholic lager
- Specialist – very rare book, appears uninterested

Pub
- Co-ordinator – music conductor, confident tone
- Team-worker – huge ears, mild, empathy
- Resource investigator – enormous mobile phone, enthusiasm, questions

Gym
- Shaper – circus announcer, whip
- Implementer – sleeves rolled up, cogs turning
- Completer/finisher – gigantic magnifying glass, detail, anxious

It also places the roles into clusters by meeting them in the:
Office: Cerebral roles   **Pub**: People roles   **Gym**: Action roles

Variation as a closer

 Ask the participants to make up their own story to illustrate the Belbin roles.

'WHAT NEXT' CLOSERS

'WHAT NEXT' CLOSERS

INTRODUCTION

As we said in the introduction, any of the activities we use can be adapted to begin or end your sessions. The following section has activities **designed with the end in mind**. The main reason is to make that dirge-like question: 'What are you going to do when you leave the course and go back to work…' a little bit more interesting.

Here are some examples.

1. Three things

Ask participants to answer these questions:
- Three things that you wanted from the course – did you get them?
- Three things that you could offer everyone else on the course – did you do that?
- Tell us three facts about yourself that you have learnt, that in some way relate to this course.

2. 'Hello, Operator!'

- Ask participants to pick a number at random from the business section of the telephone directory
- They should then phone the number and see how long they can continue the call while telling the mystery person what they intend to do differently as a result of the course
- Reward the person who manages the longest call

Variations

- Ask participants to phone their manager and tell him/her their plans.
- Ask them to phone a relative or partner or friend and tell them about the course.
- Suggest they phone the speaking clock and completely bluff the whole conversation!

3. Do me a deal

Ask delegates to pledge that within one week of a negotiation or sales course, they will have done one of the following:

- Negotiated in a high street shop
- Negotiated over the phone
- Negotiated food portions in the staff restaurant!

The point of this is to get people used to failing, so that they build their emotional robustness to failure.

4. Here is my pledge

Ask participants to make a pledge as to what they will do when they leave the course. When they have spoken, spray their pledge with Pledge (spray polish) to make it very memorable!

Caution – be careful where you spray.

5. Strike a pose

- Ask the participants before the course to take a photo of their messy desk or dysfunctional team (or whatever they have that signifies what they want to work on) and bring it to the course.
- During the introductions, ask them to share their picture with a partner by way of a visual hook to talk about what they want from the day.
- After the course, tell participants that they have to post or e-mail a picture of the new tidy desk, or their team looking jolly at a meeting, to the person they partnered during the introduction.

6. Bendy tattoo man

- Give everyone a bendy man (available from places like 'http://www.thetrainingshop.co.uk') at the end of the course
- Ask them to write the answers to certain questions on the body parts that you mention (Bic type pens work best)
- On the head, write the answer to, 'What are your thoughts?'
- On the chest, write the answer to, 'How are you feeling?'
- On the legs, write the answer to, 'What support do you need?'
- On the feet, write the answer to, 'What are your next steps?'

There is only space for small writing: key words are fine.

7. Can you tell me the way to...

- Get participants to complete an action plan saying what they are going to do when they leave the course and go back to the workplace
- Ask participants to give their plan a name which could work as a place name or tube stop
- Show them a copy of the city tube map
- Draw a new line called 'The Development Line' on the flipchart
- Include as many stops as there are participants
- Ask each of them in turn to come up to the flipchart and write the name of their plan on one of the stops
- Whilst there they should give a quick description to the rest of the group about what their 'stop' name means

Variation

Everyone draws their own tube line and the *stops* are now *steps* along the way to achieving their action plan.

8. Visible action

This closer will only work if the course is being held on the premises.

- Towards the end of your course, send the participants away to find someone from their department (preferably their manager) who can spare them ten minutes
- Participants need to tell their manager/colleague what they have learned from the course
- Participants also need to say that they have to return to the classroom in ten minutes' time, with a definite plan as to how they will use their new learning at work within the next 30 days
- They ask for the manager or colleague's help to generate the plan
- When the participants return, pair them up and allow five minutes to discuss their plans
- Review as a whole group

CLIMATE CHECKS

CLIMATE CHECKS

INTRODUCTION

Climate checks is a term that trainers have adopted to measure how people are feeling about the content of the course at any given time. At a basic level, climate checks involve asking people how they feel about the course, on a scale of 1-10. They are not particularly linked to course content. Trainers tend to use a mixture of approaches from more formal artwork through to sticking smiley faces on a flipchart.

Climate checks do allow you to carry out Kirkpatrick Level 1 feedback during the course, as part of overall validation (in case anyone asks you!).

Here are a few examples that can be used at the beginning or end of a course, or at any point during it, to open or close mini sessions.

DON'T STAND SO CLOSE TO ME

Aim
To assess level of engagement or enjoyment of course.

Materials
Whistle.

Process
1. Go outside or use a very large indoor room.
2. To start the exercise, ask everyone to stand a similar distance away from you
3. Shout out a question such as, 'How much are you enjoying the course?' and/or 'How committed are you to doing something different when you leave?'
4. Ask everyone to move, when you blow the whistle, as close to you as they feel about the answer to your question. For example, near to you if they are enjoying the course and far away if they are not.

Variations
Don't use a whistle – raise your voice and say, 'Now'.
Once people have selected their position in relation to you, ask them to go and talk to someone in a different place to find out what the differences are for them.

Warning: Be conscious of cultural differences when performing this exercise, as some people will not feel comfortable standing anywhere near you.

T-SHIRT CLIMATE

Aim
To find out what people's attitude to the course is or has been.

Materials
T-shirts (cheap, plain white T-shirts from eg Poundland or Primark).
Pens.

Process
1. Give out one T-shirt per three people.
2. Ask them to decorate the T-shirt with pictures, symbols, etc that demonstrate areas such as:
   - How they feel about the course
   - What they already know about the subject area
   - What they want from the course
3. Discuss.

Variation as a closer
Ask them to illustrate what they have learnt and what they think about the content.

MASKING YOUR FEELINGS

Aim

To provide a clear visual method of seeing what people's attitude, skills and knowledge are at the beginning and end of the course.

Materials

Masking tape, pre-prepared labels and signs, marker pens.

Process

1. Lay out three long strips of masking tape on the floor.
2. Put one label on each strip saying:
   - *Happy to be here*
   - *I know lots of stuff*
   - *I have lots of skills in this topic*
3. At one end of the masking tape put a sign reading: Ten = Lots.
4. At the other end put a sign reading: One = Little or nothing.
5. Ask delegates to put a mark on each strip of masking tape showing where they think they are in relation to the course in hand.

CLIMATE CHECKS

MARKS OUT OF TEN

Aim
Obtain instant feedback on sessions as you go through the day, or use as a very quick assessment of group consensus.

Materials
Plenty of stiff paper/card per participant or wipeable writing boards (available somewhere like Early Learning Centre or similar children's shop)

Process
1. Pre-prepare a set of cards with numbers 1-10 on for each participant.
2. At any point before, during or after you run a session, say something like, 'Marks out of ten, how did that go?' or, 'Marks out of ten, what do you know about this subject?'
3. Participants hold up the relevant number to demonstrate their feelings.

WRITE YOUR OWN ICEBREAKERS

LINKED TO CONTENT

Many people approach icebreakers like a kind of filler for their courses. We believe that there is definitely a place for them on any course to get across the style and point of the day. We also think that our learners are coming to expect more from their trainers – especially if you are an external consultant of any description.

So, here is how to write icebreakers that are entirely your own and will fit into your courses. The idea of this style is that the icebreaker gets people talking, but is also linked to the content of the course so appears seamless. There is no awkward break between the end of the icebreaker and the start of the real content.

WRITE YOUR OWN ICEBREAKERS

STEP BY STEP

To help explain the process, we have taken you through the thinking stages for one of the icebreakers, *Grow Your People*, from our first book: *Icebreakers Pocketbook*.

1. We started with a nagging feeling that we needed something new to start our coaching course with a bang!

2. We looked through all our books and resources but failed to find anything quite right. (This is always an essential part for us, as the frustration is a very positive force.)

3. We drank far too much coffee until we reached the point where anything seemed possible (it's a good idea to stop before you start to think you can scale buildings).

4. We asked, 'What exactly is the point of this course?' (It is useful here to look at your course objectives.) 'What are the key messages they must take from this course, that we can get into their heads within the first sixty minutes?'

5. We wrote down all the principles and main points that we wanted to put across to delegates. The list looked something like this:
   - GROW model
   - Taking responsibility
   - Manager's role
   - Coachee's responsibility
   - Building awareness

6. We tried to think of something that would put that across in a straightforward fashion. Nothing came to mind, so we left it alone to allow the subconscious a chance to start working.

7. Paul went to a garden centre and noticed some bulbs. It then hit him that the bulbs have to grow and need planting and caring for.

8. It seemed so obvious that we couldn't wait to get back and write it up.

9. The main message is to have fun with the topic, make it punchy and memorable and most of all, if you can link the icebreaker to the content, it is a smoother ride into the main bulk of the course. Have fun.

WRITE YOUR OWN ICEBREAKERS

PROCESS ABRIDGED

1. Decide on the objectives of the course.

2. Ask yourself what you want the learners to take away from the course (the one or two most important principles).

3. Drink unreasonable amounts of coffee.

4. Think to yourself, 'What is it like? What is it similar to?'

5. If nothing comes to you, leave it to your subconscious to come up with something.

6. When you have your idea, play around with it. Try it out on people to see if it makes sense to them.

7. When you use it, make sure you explain to people that, to you, it is symbolic of (or a metaphor for) what the course is about. This prevents the groan effect when it seems like they have something silly to do.

8. Write clear instructions of what to do and say, and follow them.

9. Be flexible when people interpret things differently from you. In our experience, people are usually much more ready to try things than you might expect.

About the Authors

Alan Evans

Alan is a high impact independent trainer.
He set up 'Made To Measure Training' in August
2003, and works with a number of trusted associates
to provide his client base (public and private sector)
with top quality learning solutions.

Cartoon by Alan Evans (shows Paul & Alan)

Alan spent several years in a trainer role with Virgin
Atlantic taking ownership of the management &
development of their Trainer Development and Personal Effectiveness programmes. His courses
are littered with illustrative cartoons, which help to make concepts memorable, stimulate thinking or
just raise a smile. He also works for the Young Enterprise Trust.

Alan can be contacted at: alan@madetomeasuretraining.co.uk

Paul Tizzard

Paul is a director of Inspirit Training Ltd, which he set up in October 2001. He is at his happiest
when living his passions of coaching, facilitating, trainer training and team developing.
Among his main clients are Virgin Atlantic, GSK, CIPD, UnumProvident and City and Guilds.

Paul can be contacted at: paul@in-spirit.co.uk
Inspirit Training Ltd, Dorking Business Centre, Haybarn House, 118 South Street, Dorking,
Surrey, RH4 2EU. Tel: 01306 644880

ORDER FORM

Your details

Name _____

Position _____

Company _____

Address _____

_____

_____

Telephone _____

Fax _____

E-mail _____

VAT No. (EC companies) _____

Your Order Ref _____

Please send me:

No. copies

The Openers & Closers Pocketbook ☐

The _____ Pocketbook ☐

The _____ Pocketbook ☐

The _____ Pocketbook ☐

The _____ Pocketbook ☐

Order by Post

MANAGEMENT POCKETBOOKS LTD

LAUREL HOUSE, STATION APPROACH, ALRESFORD, HAMPSHIRE SO24 9JH UK

Order by Phone, Fax or Internet

Telephone: +44 (0)1962 735573
Facsimile: +44 (0)1962 733637
E-mail: sales@pocketbook.co.uk
Web: www.pocketbook.co.uk

Customers in USA should contact:
Stylus Publishing, LLC, 22883 Quicksilver Drive, Sterling, VA 20166-2012
Telephone: 703 661 1581 or 800 232 0223
Facsimile: 703 661 1501 E-mail: styluspub@aol.com